D1148522

EXPLORERS WANTED!

700029058329

Also by Simon Chapman

'Thrill-a-line style...
combining fascinating fact
with sound advice'
Books for Keeps

Simon Chapman
EXPLORERS
WANTED!

In The Outback

EGMONT

EGMONT

We bring stories to life

First published in Great Britain in 2005
by Egmont Books Limited
239 Kensington High Street
London W8 6SA

Text and illustrations copyright © 2005 Simon Chapman

The moral rights of the author have been asserted

ISBN 1 4052 1835 5

1 3 5 7 9 10 8 6 4 2

A CIP catalogue record for this title
is available from the British Library

Printed and bound in Great Britain
by the CPI Group

CONTENTS

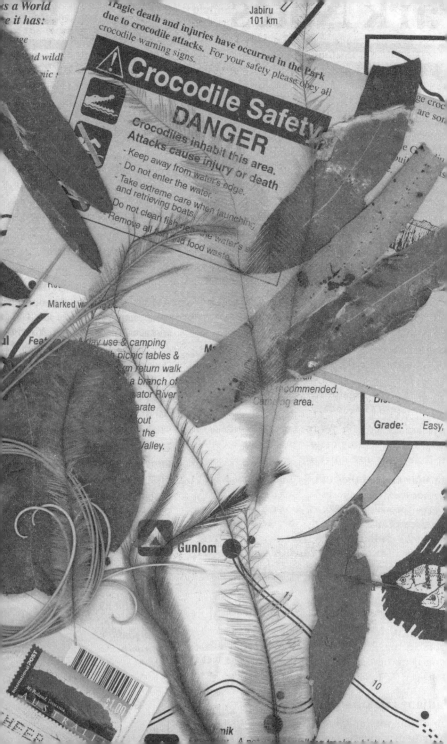

SO...YOU WANT TO EXPLORE THE AUSTRALIAN OUTBACK?

You want to ...

... Survive the searing heat and pestering flies ...?

...Discover weird and wonderful creatures ...?

...Learn to love 'bush tucker'...?

If the answer to any of these questions is **YES**,
then **Read on.**

THIS IS THE BOOK ... that will give you those vital tips for not only **how to survive** in this unforgiving country, but how to enjoy it too. Read about the explorers who came before you, how they struggled against heat, thirst and downright **dangerous wildlife**, out-back in Australia's red centre. Read on ...

YOUR MISSION:

... should you choose to accept it, is to rediscover the oolacunta desert rat-kangaroo, a wallaby reputed to be able to outrun (or out-hop!) a horse at full gallop. It's been 'discovered' twice but each time has disappeared. Last time it was seen was in 1931, when naturalist Hedley Herbert Finlayson found a colony living in the 'gibber' plains and sand ridges of Sturt's Stony Desert. Bursting with pride at his sensational find, Finlayson made further expeditions to the area to learn more about the creature which had only ever been seen nearly ninety years earlier. But when he returned in 1935, the oolacuntas had gone. Just where to nobody knew ... not until now, that is ... A group of aborigines living deep in the bush say they've seen the rat-kangaroos recently, at a place called Morangie Rocks. But you'd better get

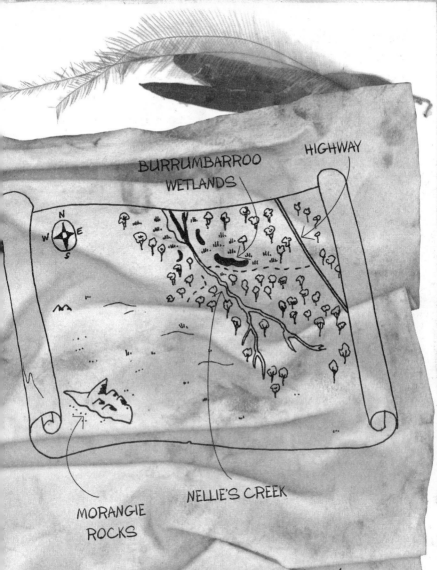

BURRUMBARROO WETLANDS

HIGHWAY

N
W   E
S

MORANGIE ROCKS

NELLIE'S CREEK

there quick, they say. Who knows when this elusive species will next move on? Will you be the one to find it before it disappears yet again?

Where will you be going?

OUTBACK

DESERTS

OUTBACK

The Outback: a vast area of bush
country, deserts and scrub that fills pretty much all of
Australia apart from the wetter and generally more habitable
areas of the far east and far west. We're talking about an
area the size of Europe that is virtually uninhabited. When
you see a road sign, you might see the next town marked on
as more than a thousand kilometres away! And don't go
thinking that the smaller towns have just been missed off.
There simply aren't any. Alice Springs is 1100km from your
destination and in between, there are just a few truck stops,
a smattering of cattle stations and several motels and shops
that cluster around the very occasional road junction. All that
way and beyond, it's usually bone dry (drier the further from
the coast you travel), searingly hot and apparently empty.
But it is not infertile. Bush fires regularly sweep across the

4

tinder-dry vegetation and when it does rain, flash floods gouge valleys across the land and fan out into shallow lakes teaming with fish and thousands of birds that have apparently sprung from nowhere. For all too brief a time, the red earth sprouts with flowers and lush vegetation, which gradually wilts, as the heat and drought set in again.

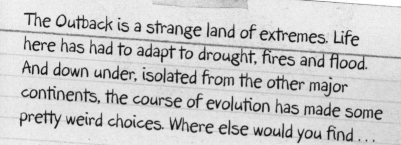

The Outback is a strange land of extremes. Life here has had to adapt to drought, fires and flood. And down under, isolated from the other major continents, the course of evolution has made some pretty weird choices. Where else would you find . . .

1. A plant-eater with the lifestyle of an antelope that hops to get around and carries its young in a pouch on its belly;

2. An ant-eating ball of spikes, which lays eggs, yet is a mammal.

3. More types of poisonous snake than anywhere else on Earth?

Can you work out what animals 1 and 2 are? There are no clues to help you.

Answers on page 9

Most, but not all, Australian mammals are marsupials. Females give birth to underdeveloped young, which they then carry around with them in a pouch of skin (usually) until they are more or less ready to fend for themselves. Many of these animals have similar lifestyles and features to mammals living on other continents.

Match the marsupial to its lifestyle and find its equivalent mammal from overseas.

Marsupial	Lifestyle (Ecological niche)	Overseas equivalent
1. Koala	A. Slow-moving tree dweller that spends much of its time asleep, digesting leaves.	W. Hedgehog (Europe)
2. Bandicoot	B. Agile meat-eater	X. Two-toed sloth (South America)
3. Northern Quoll	C. Fast-moving grass-chomper	Y. Stoat (Europe)
4. Agile Wallaby	D. Sniffing, scent-detecting insect-eater	Z. Thomson's gazelle (Africa)

Answers on page 11

But – and here's the thing – Australia is different. Comparing similar animals only gets you so far. There are no large mammal carnivores that hunt the kangaroos, nothing like the big cats on other continents. True, there may be dingo dogs (introduced about 5,000 years ago) and, until recently, wolf-like *thylacines* (the last one died in a zoo in 1936) but these do not even begin to compare on danger and scare value with lions or tigers. Also, the Australian Outback harbours no mega-herbivores like elephants or rhinos, though fossils have been found of giant wombats that chomped their way through the riverside vegetation of what is now the Northern Territories.

Late morning. Oven-hot already. The baked red earth underfoot radiates heat up at you and you can feel the sweat starting to soak your hair around the rim of your bush hat. A few flies are buzzing around your head. You know it's better to move on before more gather. Dead leaves and strips of dried tree bark scrunch noisily as you make your way forward through the clumps of dry grass and widely spaced greyish-leaved gum trees. The trunks of many of the trees are charred charcoal black at the bases, where a brush fire has raged past. Peeling bark reveals a fresh white surface, marked with raised brown lines where termites have constructed tubes that will keep out the sun while they eat away the wood beneath. You hear rustling behind a bush. Your mind races through the possibilities . . . the deadly possibilities . . .

- A **redback spider** (One bite can be fatal.) But this rustling is from something much bigger.

REDBACK

- A 2½-metre long **perentie** perhaps? (Its razor-sharp claws could do you serious harm.) Too large.

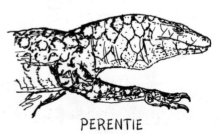

PERENTIE

- How about a deadly **taipan** snake?

Heart pounding, you stand dead still.

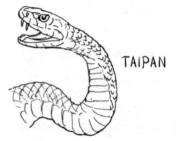

TAIPAN

8

A sheep! Yes. There are farm animals too. There are sheep and cattle stations here in the Outback that are the size of whole counties. There could be a flock of sheep nearby, maybe this one's escaped and is now running wild.

You take stock of the situation while your pulse slows to its normal rate. Just what would you do if there were a taipan in the grass at your feet? What would you do if it bit you?

You need to be properly equipped. You need to be prepared. You need some training.

ANSWERS from page 5

1. Kangaroo (or wallaby).

2. Echidna (spiny anteater).

Chapter 1
HATS WITH CORKS, DAMPER AND SWAGS

So what's with the hat? Just what are all those dangling corks for?

Flies! Not biting ones or stinging ones, these are just ordinary houseflies we're talking about. Wherever you go in the Outback it seems they are there too, buzzing around your head as soon as you stop moving, first one, then hordes of them. They can drive you to distraction. The idea of the corks is to keep them away from your face. A coarse mesh net works better; and you can wrap it around as a hatband when you don't need it.

What else will you need? The usual expedition stuff really. Your basic survival needs of food, fire, shelter and water apply as much in the Australian Outback as anywhere else in the world. You're up against hot, dry conditions, rather like in the African Savannah, so you'll be wearing the same sort of gear and take roughly the same kit.

KNIFE

SUN HAT

COMPASS

WATER BOTTLES

MEDICAL KIT

ZIP-OFF TROUSERS

STURDY BOOTS

GAITERS – PROTECTION AGAINST THORNY PLANTS AND SNAKE BITES

ANSWERS from page 6

1. A, X.	2. D, W.
3. B, Y.	4. C, Z.

Food: You might be able to find some bush tucker along the way (more about this in Chapter 7) but for the most part you'll have to carry it. In the hot climate, anything fresh will attract flies and go off quickly, so choose food that will keep. Cans and cartons of food are suitable if you have a vehicle to carry it and dried food like pasta is always useful.

Fire: Making fire is going to be the least of your worries. Just peel off some bark from any gum tree; it makes an excellent firelighter and there's usually more than enough dry wood lying around to keep your blaze going.

Shelter: The time of year that you'll be travelling, rain is highly unlikely. All you need is a swag, a bed roll consisting of a sleeping bag (or blankets), a roll mat and some fine netting you can hang over your face to keep mosquitoes away while you sleep.

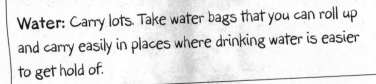

Water: Carry lots. Take water bags that you can roll up and carry easily in places where drinking water is easier to get hold of.

You'll need some transport to carry all that food and water, and over the distances involved, you're looking at pack animals or a motor vehicle to suit your needs.

Some things you could consider . . .

Camels

Before the invention of motor vehicles, camels were the ultimate Outback carriages. Load-carrying capabilities and the ability to go without water for up to a week at a time made them the transport of choice for many Australian explorers. Hundreds of camels were specially imported from Afghanistan for just this purpose. Things did not always go smoothly, however . . .

· One explorer had a camel which he called 'Rocket' because it always had such bad wind. Its insides would gurgle whenever it ate and, on the trail, it would often lift its tail and shoot out little pellets of poo, hitting the camel behind with unerring accuracy.

· One explorer was shot by his camel. He was loading his shotgun when the camel lurched and the weapon went off, blowing off one of the poor man's fingers and blasting through his cheeks. Though that was surely an accident, the camel had already gained a mean reputation after it had bitten one of the expedition party in the head.

· One explorer's camel developed sores that became so infested with maggots that they had to be emptied daily with a pint pot.

And then there's the problem of marauding wild camels. Over the years, explorers' camels were set free or sometimes escaped. And they bred. There are now over 100,000 wild camels roaming the Outback. In fact, Australia is now the only place where dromedaries (one-humped camels) live wild. The bulls (male camels) can be frisky and dangerous when they take a fancy to or want to pick a fight with the camels that are carrying your gear.

Robyn Davidson was crossing the desert from Alice Springs to the west coast in 1977, when three lustful bulls charged her caravan, frothing sticky saliva from their mouths. She shot one and drove off the others, but they returned that night, circling close to her camp. By morning, she had wounded one of them and succeeding in driving it away, but one young bull was left and while it was around she had no hope in catching 'Bub', her male camel, who, though his legs were tied, kept trying to run off. Robyn was fast becoming overheated and exhausted. She took drastic action and shot dead the last of the marauding bulls.

Motor Transport:

How about a motorbike and sidecar? This was the choice of Jack Bowers and Frank Smith on their journey around Australia in 1929. They carried a couple of spare tyres, cans for water and petrol, several guns to hunt for food along the way ... and not much else.

Notice the bike has no headlight. The pair decided it would be too dangerous to travel at night, especially as at that time few real roads had been built. Why carry the extra weight of a battery which could not be replaced in the remote areas where they were travelling? The sidecar was rather like a coffin. It held whoever wasn't driving, the tent and bedding, along with a growing collection of spears and boomerangs, which the pair traded from aboriginal hunters they met along the way.

That didn't leave much room for much petrol, however. Bowers and Smith had to rely on getting to settlements whose inhabitants could sell them enough to get to the next settlement. They also couldn't carry much food. Whenever they could, they shot bush turkeys, rabbits or kangaroos and, for the rest of the time, they lived on damper and treacle.

And what exactly is damper? The classic Australian trail food!

How to cook damper

Ingredients: 2 cups flour (self-raising is best), a pinch of salt, a spoonful of sugar (optional), some butter, 1 cup of water (or milk, or water with powdered milk).

- *Mix the dry ingredients together.*
- *Add the water/milk, kneading or stirring the mixture into dough.*
- *Shape your dough into a flattened ball.*
- *Bake in the embers of a fire for 20 minutes or so, or until you're sure it's cooked through.*

A better way to bake your damper - one where it doesn't get covered with ash and charcoal - is to put it in a billy can, then partly bury that in the embers of your fire. It helps if you grease the inside of your billy first, as otherwise the dough sticks.

This is the vehicle you've decided to bring with you, a 'Landranger' four-wheel-drive Utility 'ute' which you've named Ulysses because it sounds tough. In two-wheel-drive mode, with the engine driving just the rear wheels, Ulysses will eat up the miles on the good roads. Then you can shift into 4 WD mode and get over just about anything (we'll find out how well you handle it in Chapter 6).

Here's how you've arranged your gear in the spacious rear.

A. Water bag – top this up or refill it at every opportunity. You won't be able to rely on getting clean drinking water wherever you go.

B. Kitbag – to put your clothes and personal stuff in.

C. Spare drinking-water bottles.

D. Firewood (wrapped in a plastic sheet) – pick up dry

branches that you find lying around. Keep some in
reserve for when you are in more open or desert areas.

E. Spade.
   Knife.
F. Large plastic boxes to keep your food dust-free.
G. Tool/car spare parts in box.
H. Head torch

Keep these things at the front
of the ute for easy access:
maps, binoculars, camera, med
kit, sunglasses.

You've also had some modifications made to Ulysses the ute
to fix him up for some extreme off-roading.

Can you spot what features will help you out of the following tricky situations . . .

1. Hitting a kangaroo (this may wreck your car – and you, as well as the poor roo).

2. Driving through deep water.

3. Pulling your ute out of a gulley or sinking mud.

4. Calling for help if a snake bites you.

5. Bursting your tyres on rocky ground.

Answers on page 25

Sorted? Well, not quite. There's still one more thing you're going to take with you for that extra bit of security when you're out 'bush' . . . another ute!

Meet Cameron Noonju. He's an aborigine from the Bilingundji tribe. He's running supplies out to a cattle station close to Morangie Rocks, where his family lives. Most of his journey will be the same as yours so it makes sense for you to travel together. That way, if one of you has problems, there's going to be back-up. Unfortunately, you won't have that back-up right away. Cameron has some deliveries to make. He says he'll meet you at Nellie's Creek at the other side of the Burrumbarroo wetlands in four days' time. Call him up on the radio if there is any trouble.

No worries. How could there be? With a bush ranger like you and a ute like Ulysses!

Chapter 2
ROAD TRAINS AND DIDGERIDOOS

Midday. The thing about Australian bush roads, you soon realise, is that they are very long and very straight. Virtually no one lives along them and, at times, it seems that virtually no one drives along them. You have to keep up your concentration or else your mind drifts and your tyres end up kicking up the stones on the verges, as you slowly lose your line of travel.

The red line on your map makes this line of tarmac and gravel look like some major artery, but all you've passed is a couple of turn-offs to farms 30 or 40 kilometres from the highway and one petrol stop some way back. It's not as if the scenery has been all that varied; widely spaced, straggly trees with blackened trunks and greyish leaves, with long, yellow grass in between. The only wild animal you've seen so far was some sort of wallaby and that was roadkill. It had attracted a gaggle of carrion-eating kites that scattered as you drove past. You could see wedge-tailed eagles

WEDGE-TAILED EAGLE

KITES

riding high on the hot thermal clouds above and, in the far distance, a cloud of dust .. which is getting bigger . . .

A dust storm?
A whirlwind perhaps?
Then you see the huge bull bars, the vast cab and the four trailers . . .

BBLAARR-RR-RR-OOOOO!

The pressure wave as it passes knocks your ute sideways. Momentarily, you are showered with gravel and blinded in a dust storm. That was what they call a 'road train'; all the carrying capacity of four normal lorries combined into one unstoppable mega-truck. That's how Australians transport goods through the vast emptiness that is the Outback.

You knock Ulysses back into gear and hit the road again, wary now for any road train dust-clouds you see on the horizon. You feel quite some relief when you turn off on to the narrow track that your map shows. You will skirt round the edge of the Burrumbarroo Wetlands to Nellie's Creek, where you've arranged to meet Cameron. At least on this small track there'll be no chance of being wiped out by rogue road trains. The downside is that this dirt road is rutted with deep tyre tracks and cratered with potholes. You send up a cloud of dust behind you as you drive and are convinced Ulysses will quickly shake to pieces unless you drive much, much slower.

From time to time as you bump and bounce forward, you pass knobbly pillars of dried earth or rock sticking out of the grass at the side of the track. Some are twice the height of your car and splay out into vertical 'flutings' near to the top. Others further on are much lower and spiky cone-shaped but, like the fluted 'cathedral' mounds, they are always the same colour as the soil they sprout from - sometimes a really bright brick-red orange.

CATHEDRAL MOUNDS

The grey mounds you come to on a low-lying plain of grassland a little further on are the weirdest of all. It's like

you're driving through a graveyard. Each mound is like a concrete paving slab and each lines up in exactly the same direction; due north.

So just what is going on? What are these structures and why do they have such strange shapes?

These are termite mounds; the homes of ant-sized insects that have cemented together millions of particles of earth to build these structures. Colonies of millions live here:

· Mostly small **workers** that forage for grass or wood in the cool of the night (protozoa microbes in their guts help them digest this tough stuff).

· To protect them, there are **soldiers** with acid squirter mouthparts, and somewhere in the middle is . . .

· One **queen**, an egg-laying machine as long as your finger that cannot move and pumps out eggs each day.

WORKERS

SOLDIERS

QUEEN

· There are also winged males and females (queens in waiting) too, called **alates**. It's their job to fly off and set up new colonies.

WINGED ALATE

KING (WINGS FALLEN OFF)

In the Australian bush it's termites that are the major herbivores. Forget kangaroos and wallabies. Weight for weight, there are tons of termites for every roo.

Termites have soft bodies that dry easily in the daytime and make good eating for animals like echidnas. The mounds, where cool air circulates, offer a sanctuary for their sensitive inmates. Tunnels flow from ground level to deep underground (sometimes several metres), where the temperature never really changes. With its cooling air currents and constant humidity, you can think of a termite mound as an insect air-conditioning system.

But what's with the different shapes of the mounds?

Cathedral mounds are on land that never floods. They are the largest and can extend metres underground too. Where you get the right conditions, you often see these spaced every twenty metres or so around the bush.

The spiky, often cone-shaped, mounds belong to flood plain termites in grassland that is submerged for part of the year. There's no point in the termites here digging their galleries underground because the mounds will fill with water.

ANSWERS from page 18

1. Roo bars   2. Snorkel   3. Winch
4. Radio   5. Spare wheels

The north-facing termite mounds are a special type of flood plain mound that is lined up to heat up or cool down depending on the direction of the sun during the day. It works like this:

The sun rises in the east = side on to the slab = maximum heating up... Because of the Earth's rotation, the sun is in the north at midday = edge on to the slab = least heating. In the afternoon, with sun moving round to the west the other side heats up. The result is that over the course of the day, the inside temperature of the termite mound stays more or less constant.

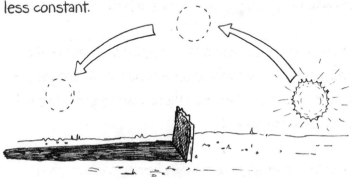

These mounds are called **magnetic mounds** because of the way they point north like compass needles. There's nothing magnetic about them though, and nor are the worker termites that build them particularly clever. They just build their mounds to stay as cool as possible. In fact, if there's a regular cooling wind on one side, they may not face north at all.

Tree-piping termites and didgeridoos

When you gather fallen wood for tonight's campfire, take a closer look. Many of the branches you find will be hollow, bored into tubes by termites that specialise in eating wood, living and dead. Aboriginal wind instruments called didgeridoos are made from termite-hollowed branches.

HOLLOW LOG

HOW TO GET A SOUND OUT OF A DIDGERIDOO

The trick is in the breathing.
· Blow a low-pitched raspberry down the tube.
· You'll get a low droning trumpeting.
· To keep the note going without running out of breath, breathe out of your mouth, taking breaths through your nose at the same time.
· This is called circular breathing.
  Getting the knack of it is
  very difficult.

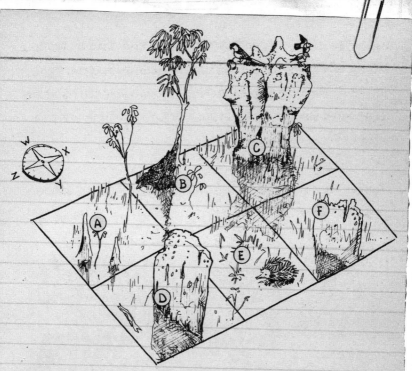

Look at this area of the bush. Which square . . .

1. Is never flooded during the year?

2. Contains an animal that eats termites?

3. Contains animals that use termite mounds to provide housing?

4. Would provide what you need to make a didgeridoo?

5. Which direction is north? W, X, Y or Z?

Answers on page 29

Your daydreams of termite architecture end abruptly by the strong smell of wood-smoke in your nostrils. To your right, smoke is billowing above the trees, though you can't see any flames that would indicate a bush fire. You pull the ute to a stop and assess the situation.

Look at the clues and decide on the best course of action.

WIND DIRECTION

BURNT GROUND

BUSH FIRE

- You are currently heading westwards.
- The wind direction is northwest-southeast.
- The smoke direction is north, where you can also see kites (birds of prey) dive-bombing the ground. The bush ahead is charred and blackened at ground level.
- Immediately to the south of the road, lush tall green grass is growing. (You spot a small grey and white heron taking off from there.)

Smoke is heading your way. You are now sure you can see orange flames licking round the feet of those gum trees.

North, east (back the way you came), south or west?

Which way will you go? Make your decision and find out whether you made the right choice in the next chapter . . .

ANSWERS from page 27

1. SQUARE C. Cathedral termite mound.

2. SQUARE E. Echidna: along with platypuses, echidnas are monotremes - mammals that lay eggs!

3. SQUARE C. Hooded parrot, double-barred finch. Termite mounds provide homes (and hunting grounds) for a variety of animals like goannas, quolls (a cat-like marsupial carnivore) and pythons.

4. SQUARE B. Tree piping termites

5. Direction W.

Chapter 3
BUSH FIRE

Drive on, and get a move on! (**West** was the way to go.)

The bush fire has already swept over that scorched ground ahead and is unlikely to do so again, especially as the wind will soon blow the flames through the dry grass around and behind you (east). Ahead of the flames, the kites are swooping on lizards and bush rats flushed out into the open. For them, a fire is a hunting opportunity too good to miss. It's said that kites will even snatch up burning twigs and drop them further on to spread the blaze and so provide them with a bigger menu to choose from.

BLACK KITE

As for the other choices, north would have taken you right into the fire. South would get you bogged down in a marsh - reeds and a water bird were a giveaway there.

You trundle forward, past some smouldering tussocks of grass and into unburnt country again. From what you saw of the fire, it was only actually a thin line that was burning, a fire 'front' that raced through the dry grasses and left the trees slightly charred around the bases but otherwise unharmed. This was what they call a 'cool' burn and it was probably started by humans. Here's why and how.

Most of the trees here are types of eucalyptus - also known as gum trees. With their flaky bark and oily sap, these are trees that are positively designed to burn - or rather their bark is.

PEELING BARK

It falls off in strips littering the ground with natural firelighters, ready for some lightning strike to set them ablaze. The fire that then sweeps through is fast-burning and usually does little more damage to the gum trees than singeing the trunks; and the tree reacts by shedding that bark. The fire has opened up the gum-tree seeds, which are now ready to sprout on the nutrient-rich ash when it next rains. What's more, the new seedlings will sprout on cleared ground free of those pesky other plants that would otherwise have got in the way of the sunlight.

So, where do people fit into the picture?

They start most of the fires - and have been doing so for thousands of years. The aborigines first appeared on the scene around 60,000 years ago, arriving, it is thought, from Asia. They soon discovered that burning off areas of bush at certain times of year (like just after the end of the rainy season when the fires wouldn't spread too much) would encourage fresh grass to grow and that would attract kangaroos and wallabies, which they hunted for meat. Over time, the Australian natural landscape was transformed. Forests gave way to more open bush country and kangaroos and grassland animals became more common. The Outback exists because of the aboriginal people and their fire and in turn aboriginal culture depends on the Outback (as we shall see in Chapter 7).

But what do you know about gum trees of the Australian bush? Possibly very little. Read these questions and see if you can work out the answers.

Gum Tree Quiz

1. Many gum trees are named after their flammable bark. Work out from their names which one of these trees has bark that won't easily set alight.

a. Woolybutt

b. Stringy-bark

c. Iron-bark

d. Candle-bark

2. Gum trees come in many beautiful shades. You come
   across some trees with pinkish-orange trunks. They are:

a. Salmon gum

b. Ghost gum

c. Red River gum

d. Snow gum

GHOST GUMS

3. What caused the 'scribbles' on this scribbly gum?

a. People doodling

b. Insect grubs under the bark

c. Nibbling kangaroos

d. Smouldering embers from bushfires

SCRIBBLY GUM

4. Rainbow lorikeets are purple and orange
   parrots with brush-like bristles on their
   tongues. What do they feed on?

a. Gum nuts which they crack open
   with their beaks

b. Gum-tree bark, which they prize off
   with their beak's hooked tip.

LORIKEET

c. Insects which they brush off the branches

d. Sugary, liquid nectar which they brush out of
   gum-tree flowers.

5. Galahs are pink cockatoos (also members of the parrot family). They have powerful beaks but do not have brush tongues. What do they eat?

a. Gum nuts which they crack open with their beaks.

b. Gum-tree bark, which they prize off with their beaks' hooked tip.

c. Insects which they brush out of the branches.

d. Sugary, liquid nectar, which they brush out of gum-tree flowers.

6. Over years of growing, the trunks of many eucalypts become hollowed out inside. This is because of:

a. Nesting kookaburras

b. Termites

c. Nibbling kangaroos

d. Smouldering embers from bush fires

7. Which of these animals only eats eucalyptus leaves?

a. Koala

b. Kangaroo

c. Termite

d. Quoll

Answers on page 37

The terrain is opening out. The track you're driving on was obviously fairly recently part of the wide expanse of wetland. In the bare, dried-up edges you can see deep tyre ruts where, until recently, this was soft mud. A couple of metres up the trunks and branches of the trees there is a tide line of matted dead reeds, which shows how high the water came several months earlier.

Now the billabong (lake) is drying up. In its centre, it's more of a swamp than a lake, with few patches of open water between the tall marsh grasses and round lily pads. Here, it's as if all the water birds that were once spread over the wide wetland are now concentrated into the tiny space in the middle, all competing for the bonanza of frogs, fish and other animals that are trapped in the shrinking lake.

MAGPIE GOOSE

There are thousands of whistling ducks lining the muddy edges, V-shaped skeins of magpie geese that fly in from time to time, multiple varieties of herons and cormorants, swooping sea eagles and huge black-necked jabiru storks that sweep the shallow water with

JABIRU STORK

their butcher-knife beaks. They snap up any living thing they come into contact with and you notice that while the jabirus are sweep-snapping, all the other birds stay well out of the way.

It's an idyllic scene – perfect for a campsite. There's water and a pleasantly cool breeze to blow away flies and mosquitoes, and ample wood for your campfire. You gather some fallen branches and, for tinder to light your fire, you pull off some paper bark from the marsh-side *melaleuca* trees. Soon you have a mass of glowing coals to bake your damper on. You've laid out your swag to one side and you're looking forward to the perfect sunset that's due any moment.

Just one thing would make it perfect. A good cup of tea. Grasping your billycan, you wade barefoot through the soft mud at the edge of the billabong right up to the water's edge. As you fill the pot and watch the evening waterfowl fly past, you know that nothing could possibly ruin the atmosphere . . .

Not even the log that's floating towards you . . .

The log that's just sunk . . .

And maybe it was just a trick of the evening light or something, but there was something about that log.

You could have sworn it had eyes!

ANSWERS from pages 32-34

1. C. The others all burn really well. Iron bark protects against the flames of bush fires and unlike the other types doesn't peel off.

2. A. Ever heard of salmon pink? That's the colour of salmon gums.

3. B.

4. D. Some types of possum and fruit bats also are rather partial to eucalyptus nectar.

5. A. Not just galahs; other types of cockatoo too.

6. B.

7. A. The leaves make pretty poor food. To digest them and get rid of the poisons in them, koalas need to sleep for up to 20 hours each day. Koalas only live in forests where they can get hold of several different types of gum-tree leaves, so that their diet gives them enough nutrients. Koalas don't live in the Outback but in the forests of Eastern and Southern Australia.

Chapter 4
SALTY CROCS

A log submerges. It has eyes. You know what this means.

Saltwater Crocodile, the ultimate predator of these wetlands, and at up to 8 metres long, a carnivore of dinosaur proportions. Its head is as long as a grown man's legs, with jaws that can snap shut with enough force to crush a buffalo's skull. A mere swipe from its tail would easily knock you senseless.

And it's hunting **YOU!**

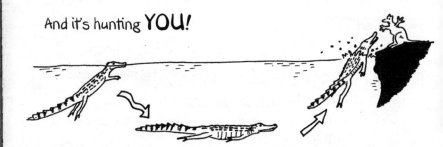

Floating in the water, with just its nostrils and eyes above the surface, it spotted you filling up your billycan. Now it has submerged, having memorised your position, and is propelling itself forward with its rudder-like tail. Finally . . .

(It's definitely time to move. **NOW!**)

. . . comes the lunge. The croc leaps upwards and forwards – up to a couple of metres – and snaps at its prey.

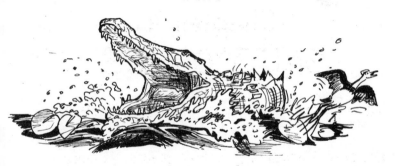

Phew! That was close - though perhaps that was only a half-hearted attempt. After a good feed, a salty croc doesn't need to eat for several weeks and perhaps your croc wasn't that hungry.

Crouching there at the edge of the billabong, you were easy meat. A large salty can crunch a buffalo, so you would have been no problem. If it had got you, you might have been dragged under and left decaying for a while, perhaps under a submerged log (rotting flesh is easier to rip off). Sometimes salties go for other crocodiles (usually smaller ones). They bite off the heads and tails and leave the bodies as the stomachs contain bone-dissolving stomach acid, which could cause them harm. Though salties do hunt kangaroos, birds and just about anything that comes down to the waterside, most of the time they go for much simpler fare.

70 per cent of a large croc's diet is made up of mud crabs, while their babies prefer insects and crustaceans (crabs, prawns, crayfish and the like).

Salties aren't the only crocs living around here. There are also **freshies** - freshwater crocodiles. Unlike their fierce cousins, they live on fish, are generally smaller and are much safer to be around. You can swim in their river and they generally won't go for you (unless you provoke them). Saltwater crocodiles, however (even fairly small ones), can be bad news. Here's how to tell the two types apart:

SALTWATER CROCODILE

Size. Freshwater crocodiles are generally smaller. They only grow up to around 2 1/2 metres so anything bigger must be a salty.

FRESHWATER CROCODILE

Snout. Thin toothy snout = freshy (for snapping fish). Wide bone-crunching conk = salty.

Choice of river. Fresh-water pond (billabong) or river only for freshwater crocodiles? And salt-water only for saltwater crocodiles? Unfortunately no. They're quite happy to hang around in freshwater rivers and billabongs too, as well as estuaries and coastal mangrove swamps. Generally, freshies range much further inland, though if the water level has risen really high in a particularly rainy season, salties can end up just about anywhere – in city drains, walking down the streets, they've even been found in people's gardens!

So, if there are saltwater crocodiles in this river, how do you go about getting the water you need?
The answer is *very carefully*. Scan the banks and the water ahead for signs . . .

- Is there the trail-dragging slipway in the mud where a croc has recently entered the water? If there are marks and the mud isn't yet dry, it's only just gone in.
- Can you see a croc? Or more likely just the top of its head? If there is a freshwater croc nearby, chances are there won't be any salties there too and you can fetch water safely (salties eat freshies if they get the chance but freshies are more agile).

If in doubt, it's probably better not to chance it. Use some water from your reserve water bags onboard Ulysses. Make camp away from the billabong edge where there's less of a crocodile hazard. You can probably find somewhere safer to refill your water store later on.

BLACK
COCKATOOS

Morning. You wake up to the raucous **breeyeek, breeyeek** calls of a flock of red-tailed black cockatoos in the trees around your camp. No saltwater crocodile has slithered up from the billabong to bother you. The only disturbance to your camp has been caused by a blue-winged kookaburra that swooped down from a low branch and made off with the bacon rashers you were about to fry up for breakfast. Today you must drive on from this idyllic billabong and rendezvous with Cameron Noonju at Nellie's Creek. You'll need his help to find the *oolacunta* rat-kangaroo in the dusty Outback beyond this gum-tree country. You

KOOKABURRA

decide to forget the stolen bacon and set off along the track before the sun rises high and it gets really hot.

Later. The road you are driving on is becoming narrower and much rougher. Soon the baked-mud surface gives way to a tyre-rutted track little wider than your truck. You have to weave around other people's deep tyre tracks, scraping past bushes that have started to grow over the road. You avoid tree trunks that jut out and keep out of the really deep ruts where your wheels would almost certainly become lodged.

Often, you have to veer up on to hardened mud ridges with the jeep lurching alarmingly. Other times you're forced to avoid the track entirely and cut straight through the bush. But watch out! Jagged tree stumps and termite mounds can cause serious damage if you crash into them.

Where the road flattens out again it is tempting to drive fast here. The road has become corrugated as vehicles have sped down this section. You can avoid some of the constant jarring by upping your speed. Again, watch out. These bits can become treacherous. Under the top layer of dust is smooth clay. At any turn, your wheels may slide. Luckily it's not wet; then it would be like a skidpan.

Snake! Stop! As you slam on the brakes, the cloud of dust trailing behind you catches up and for a few moments it's as though you're in your own brown cloud.

The dust settles.

Dead ahead in the road, two grey-brown snakes, each about a metre long, are locked in some sort of fight. They twist around and over each other, grappling for supremacy. Sometimes they rear up as high as your headlights. They are totally unconcerned by your presence. You can't go forwards without running them over and, here, there are too many trees to consider driving off-road. You get a stick with the intention of shoving them out of the way . . .

Is this wise? Two steps out of the car, reaching for that stick, the two snakes are an arm's length from your face. You stop to reconsider.

One-metre-long.
Grey-brown. Those little cogs of your memory are whirring into action.

Brown snake?
        Fierce snake?
                Mulga snake?
                        Death Adder?
                                Taipan?

Chapter 5
TAIPAN

You've never been quite so still in all your life. It's as if time has stopped. You observe every movement each snake makes; every twist, every loop, every flick of the tongue, aware of the dryness in your mouth and your racing pulse. It's like you're viewing the scene from above and can sense even the slightest movement, exactly as it happens.

The world's ten most poisonous snakes all live in Australia. These ones right in front of you could be deadly taipans or mulga snakes, for all you know. Their colouring does not make identification easy either. Venomous brown snakes, taipans, fierce snakes and mulga snakes can all be around this size and colour. So can several non-poisonous types. The only way to find which types you are dealing with would be to look at the way their belly scales are arranged - but let's face it, are you really going to crawl up that close to them to have a look? Just back away - slowly - get in the ute, watch the two males' spectacular bout and hope they'll be finished soon.

In the meantime, here are some things you should know about the most deadly Australian snakes - think of it as a sort of top five rundown.

SNAKE CHART RUNDOWN

Just in at number 5 is **eastern tiger**. Not as poisonous as a fierce snake (no. 6), it makes up for that by biting people far more frequently.

A new entry at number 4: **eastern brown snake**. Highly poisonous and easy to anger, but its venom glands don't hold that much.

At number 3, with many bites on record and a name to inspire terror, is **death adder**.

Hanging in there at number 2 is **mulga snake**. Though its poison is the weakest of this top 5, its stores of venom are the largest around. And when mulga snake bites, it chews too, to make sure its poison is a real hit.

 But still at the top is **taipan**! With its combination of long fangs, potent poison and fierce temper, it's definitely the most dangerous snake around.

The thing to understand is that being the most poisonous doesn't necessarily make you the most dangerous. That depends on factors such as how easy you are to annoy, how common you are and whether you live in the sorts of places where people actually go. For instance, fierce snakes have far more deadly poison than mulga snakes but living in really remote areas, they are considered less dangerous because few people ever come across them, let alone get bitten.

Also consider this: even though the ten most deadly snakes live in Australia, there are very few deaths from their bites. Why is this? Antivenin (snake-bite medicine). Australian snakes are well studied and hospitals are stocked up with drugs which can counter the effect of the poisons. This means that if you can get to hospital reasonably quickly after being bitten, you are pretty likely to live. Worldwide, snakes such as cobras and vipers in parts of Africa and India kill far more people, as there simply isn't the access to the correct medical treatment.

Here's what snakebites can do to you . . .

All the really poisonous Australian snakes have venom that contains chemicals called neurotoxins. 'Neuro' means 'nervous', as in nervous system . . . so these are poisons that affect your nervous system – your internal wiring that passes messages from your brain to the rest of your body and relays messages from your senses back to your brain. Basically, neurotoxins block these messages; for instance like the one telling your lungs to keep breathing. A taipan bites you and that message gets blocked. You are paralysed. You suffocate.

Still, if you do get bitten, here's what you should do.

1. Don't wash off the venom. If you can get to a hospital, the staff there will take a swab and use a special indicator chemical to work out which type of snake bit you. Then they can give you the right antivenin.

2. Bind an elastic bandage firmly around the whole of the limb affected to slow the poison's spread. Snake venom does not travel quickly through your bloodstream; it moves more slowly through the tiny tubes of the lymph system. Don't wrap your bandage too tightly, as you mustn't cut off your blood supply. That would make things far worse.

3. Stay calm (yes, you have to). Drink plenty of fluids. Radio out or send someone to get help.

But what if you're alone in the middle of nowhere, with no chance of rescue coming? The only thing you can do is to take heart from the fact that:

A. the snake that bit you may not be poisonous and

B. even if it was poisonous, it may have given you a 'dry' bite (no poison) or not injected a full dose into you. The chances are you're not going to feel too well, but probably you won't die.

Eventually, tired of waiting for the snakes to finish their wrestling match, you edge the ute forwards, pulling it as far off the track as you can manage without hitting a tree.

Late afternoon. Crossing a dried-up creek.

Here is your first real challenge in the ute, one you'll need to put the gears into 4-wheel drive for. You'll have to somehow roll down the steep bank without tipping over, cross the creek at the bottom without sinking in the mud or lodging on the boulders, then negotiate the steep mud ramp on the other side. Time to shift gear. Pull that smaller gear stick to the left of the main one backwards into 4Lo. That means all four wheels will have engine power and the gearing will be really low. Maximum traction, the engine will rev really fast. You won't be able to move the vehicle fast but it will provide a large force for when you go uphill.

Let's split the crossing into sections. Also look at the *clinometer*. This tells you what angle slope you're on.

CLINOMETER

Sideways, your ute can manage a 45-degrees slope before rolling over. On 4Lo gearing it will get up a 45-degrees slope if the surface is firm.

Look at the picture and decide your route. You can only drive through sections that touch next to each other. So you could drive Q to W or Q to X for example, but not Q to V as those two sections aren't touching.

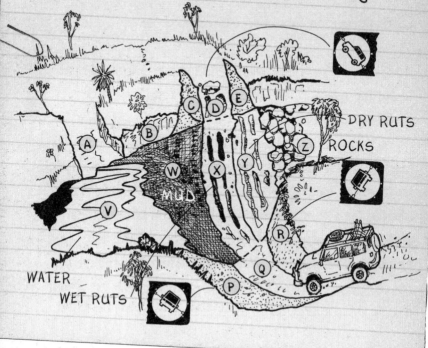

DRY RUTS

ROCKS

MUD

WATER
WET RUTS

Let's see if you can power your way across.

Divide your planned route into start, middle and end. Remember your choice and let's see how you do. Keep track of your score. If you go down to zero or below, your car has become hung-up on rocks, bogged down or toppled on its side. Below zero means you've not only become stuck, you've damaged your vehicle too.

First Section: Down into the creek.

Section	Points	Comments
P	1	Slow-going, you nearly topple.
Q	2	Hold the steering wheel loosely, but stay in full control. You have to let the ute find its own way down the steep slope.
R	0	Didn't you notice the angle of the slope? You tip the ute on to its side. Oh dear. You are stuck in a probably crocodile-infested creek-bed. You will need help to get out of this situation. You fail this activity.

Second Section: The crossing

Section	Points	Comments
V	-1	With your snorkel, your engine will keep running but your wheels sink in to the soft mud underneath. This is prime saltwater-crocodile habitat. Do you really want to get out?
W	-1	Look again at the picture. Notice the vehicle tracks going into the mud and coming out but not in the section that you are trying to cross. That's because the mud here is really soft. Depending which way you came down the bank, you are now progressing slowly or bogged down.
X	-1	Those wheel ruts are full of water and you should know that underneath is thick mud. Again, depending which way you came down the bank, your progress is slow or you are now bogged down.
Y	0	By keeping on the hard, dried mud above the wheel ruts, you can keep going – slowly.
Z	-2	The rocks here are simply too big for you to cross. If you tried, you will quickly have become stuck.

Third section: Up the opposite bank

Section	Points	Comments
A	0	The easiest route up, though hard to get to.
B	-2	That's a vertical cliff, you fool! There's no way up.
C	-1	You might just make it, but there's a high risk of rolling over.
D	-2	Though it looks the most direct route, the big rock with the pothole would stop your vehicle in its tracks or cause damage.
E	0	By no means easy, but possible.

Your Score

Above zero: You made it. (2 is the best score. If you drove the route QYE you made it across easily. QXE and QWA will both succeed with a score of 1.)

Zero. You got stuck. Radio for help or hope some other vehicle will turn up and tow you out.

Below Zero. Not only did you get stuck, but you damaged your ute too.

Assuming you made it across, you rev your way up the bank and out of the river channel - and guess who you come across on the other side? Yes, it's Cameron. He's got a fire going and is cooking yams in glowing charcoals at the edge. He waves you over as if it's only been two minutes not two days since he last saw you.

He says he's heard more about those rat-kangaroo *oola-whatsits* that you're looking for over by Morangie Rocks, out in the desert country. According to an aboriginal tribesman he met yesterday, the roos were there last week but they may have moved on. They're said to run like the wind. Even if you get to Morangie, you may never catch up with the little critters to prove their existence.

If your score is zero you have become stuck. Ask yourself if you are really cut out to continue with the mission.

Chapter 6
KANGEROOS OF THE RED CENTRE

Early next morning. You in your ute, Ulysses, led by Cameron in his pick-up, are bumping across a vast scorched plain towards an orange stone escarpment on the skyline.

You keep your car windows tightly shut to keep out the clouds of red dust that billow out behind you and to get the maximum cooling effect from Ulysses' fans. The desert scrub is featureless apart from the odd mulga tree and clumps of spiky spinifex grass that dot the rust-coloured earth.

Red Centre

The heart of Australia is sometimes called the Red Centre. Here's why:

The red colour is caused by iron oxide (rust) concentrating on the surface. Each time it rains, the water seeps into the earth, mixing the iron oxide and silica (sand). The heat of the dry season evaporates surface water and draws up the moisture that's deeper down. Iron oxide is pulled up with the moisture. It coats grains of sands on the surface and hardens as the water carrying it evaporates. Over years of this happening, a crust of reddish-coated nodules of sand builds up and the surface looks rust red.

WATER EVAPORATING

WATER WITH IRON OXIDE DRAWN UP

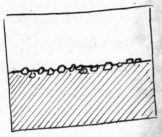

IRON OXIDE-COVERED NODULES AND CRUST ON SURFACE

The hours pass. The kilometres go by. You're daydreaming about where to turn in for the night, what food you can cook and whether should you call Cameron up on the radio, when . . . oh!

Phew, that was close! Some inner sense saved you, made you step on the brake just in time. Was that a kangaroo? When you swerved, it must've jumped clean over the road. You can see it bounding away, head held low, thick tail bouncing down and up in time with each effortless jump. It's a big 'red', nearly as tall as you when it stands up. There are more nearby on either side of the road. Some are smaller – younger? And you can see one that's definitely fatter. Is that a joey peeping out of its pouch?

Kangaroos – so familiar, so typical of the Australian bush, but how much do you really know about them? In many ways, the way they live – munching grass in dry savannahs and semi-deserts – is not unlike the lifestyles of some African antelopes. Some features like the grass-grinding teeth and wide-angle vision are very similar, yet the overall design is totally different. For a start, kangaroos are marsupials – animals with pouches – and further, they jump on two legs, not run on four.

Design features

Flexible tendons in legs. As the kangaroo lands, these store energy, ready to use on the next jump. An adult male red kangaroo can jump 9 metres along and clear fences over 2 metres high. Its top speed is 60-70 kph. A kangaroo jumping uses less energy than an antelope running. It also is a very convenient means of travel for an animal with its young in a belly pouch.

Counter-balancing tail. This flexes up and down as the roo hops, keeping it balanced and also giving it extra *oomph* as it bounces.

Fantastic child-rearing ability. The joey in its pouch is just one of three young 'on the go' at any time. This older joey spends much of its time out and usually only puts its head inside to take a slurp of milk from time to time. Meanwhile, attached to another teat, is a barely formed embryo. This was born before it had even developed hind legs. It had to crawl its way up its mother's belly and latch on to a teat to continue its development. The milk it drinks has a different formulation to that drunk by its older brother or sister.

Meanwhile, there's another fertilised egg 'on hold' in the womb. Once joey number one is ready to face the outside world, that egg will then continue its development and that will mean the mother is ready to mate and have another egg cell fertilised.

This way, kangaroos can raise young very quickly indeed (235 days from fertilised egg to out of the pouch and away). That's why, after a drought that causes many to die, kangaroo numbers *bounce back* as soon conditions (such as rain and having more grass to eat) are better.

KANGAROO QUIZ

Think you know a bit about kangaroos now? Try this quick quiz. Answer **true** or **false**.

1. Small types of kangaroos are called wallabies.

2. If you cross a kangaroo with a wallaby you get a *wallaroo*.

3. Most old kangaroos die of starvation.

4. If you saw a kangaroo licking its forearms, it would be trying to cool itself.

5. Farmers clearing bush land for cattle and sheep to graze on has caused kangaroo numbers to increase.

6. Killer kangaroos have been known to prey on people.

Answers on page 66

And what about this *oolacunta* desert rat-kangaroo you're trying to find? Is it just like any other type of kangaroo? The answer is basically yes, except that it is small and is said to have a strange way of hopping – with the right foot landing in front of the left, not both feet together, as with other kangaroos. And from what its discoverer Finlayson said in 1935, *oolacuntas* are fast. They outran his horses, keeping a pace of 20 kph up for three hours at a time. So look out for rabbit-sized, lop-sided hoppers racing at full pelt!

The rough drive goes on for hour after hour. Yours and Cameron's trucks are tiny dots on a vast, red plain, with the Morangie Rocks ever in the distance through the shimmering heat hazes. In some places there are track-marks from other vehicles that you follow. Elsewhere, you have to thread your way forwards through the tussocks of grass, avoiding bare patches of sand where you know your wheels would sink in. The reason you and Cameron are driving two vehicles is for security. If one of you cracks an axle, bursts a tyre, overheats or breaks the car in some other way, there is always the other to help you out of the situation. Hopefully, you need never get into the dire situation that befell explorer Ernest Giles in 1874.

Dying for a wallaby: A story of survival against the odds

Ernest Giles wished he had a camel instead of the four horses that he and his companion, Gibson, had brought with them to cross the scrubland. Already, because of lack of water, they had had to set two of their animals loose, hoping that somehow they would make it back to their base camp 160 kilometres away (they didn't). The explorers' drinking water situation worsened when Giles's mare, crazed with thirst, bit one of the remaining water bags, forcing out its cork and spilling out its contents all over the bare earth.

The next day, when Gibson's horse keeled over and died, it became clear that the pair would never get to the ridge they could see in the distance. They agreed that Gibson should take the remaining horse, Giles's compass and most of the water, and go back for help.

No water left, no horse, alone; Giles knew that 50 kilometres back was where he and Gibson had left a stash of food and water — several skin bags and a barrel — for the return journey. If he could get back there, Giles reckoned, then he might survive.

It was hard but he made it. His relief at finding the supply dump soon turned to dismay though. Gibson had taken all of the food except a few half-rotten strips of dried horse flesh that were left at the bottom of one of the sacks. Also he had taken the small water skins and left only the barrel. Now that was the only water container that Giles had. How was he going to lug that across the desert?

Giles set off again back to his original base camp but his progress under the weight of the barrel was pitiful. He stumbled through spiky spinifex grass, sometimes as high as himself, which stuck in his clothes and ripped his skin. Soon his arms and legs were a painful mass of infected cuts. Whenever he tried to rest in the shade of any trees he found, he was set upon by bulldog ants, which jabbed him with wasp-like stings. Once he found the tracks of Gibson's (his own!) horse, but they led in the wrong direction. Giles decided not to follow them.

Giles's situation was desperate. There were times when he lost consciousness. He might have been out for minutes, hours or even days.

In his dazed state, he did not know. Just when he was ready to give up, to lay down and die, Giles had his lucky break.

He found a baby wallaby – presumably abandoned by its mother – and ate it whole – fur, bones – all of it in one go (Giles later said it was delicious). That wallaby gave him the strength to carry on and to make it back to his base camp.

As for Giles's companion, he was never seen again. These days however, it is his name not Giles's that is remembered. The area where this story happened is now known as the 'Gibson Desert'.

Don't let this happen to you. Stick close to Cameron. Stay together. You may even get some good food for supper. He's promised you some 'bush tucker' when you make camp tonight, though hopefully not baby wallaby with the skin and fur left on.

The sun is setting by the time the two of you make it to the rocks. You park up the utes and Cameron leads you up a gentle climb to a great slanted overhang that glows warm orange in the horizontal rays.

The sunlit slab is covered in paintings, every one daubed in earthy colours: yellow and red ochre, white and black. There are outlines of hands, and pictures of people, kangaroos and lightning storms. The strange thing about the animal pictures is that they seem to show the bones, a bit like an x-ray image. Some pictures are drawn on top of others as if later artists ran out of space and had to start recycling the area available.

These pictures could be modern or hundreds of years old. Aboriginal culture goes back 60,000 years - it's the longest continuous human culture on Earth. These pictures celebrate hunting and gathering and the stories of the gods and Earth spirits in the 'dreamtime' - the mythic past when the Earth and its animals and plants were formed.

ROCK ART

One small image shows a tiny kangaroo with its feet placed one before the other. The *oolacunta*? You're just considering this when Cameron gently tugs your arm and says to make camp down by the cars. He'll be back in a while with tea. Then he slips off into the dusk, leaving you alone with the night noises. You can hear a *curleeeooo* cry of some bird, a distant yelping and, nearby, what sounds like a dog barking in the bushes above your camp. Is it a dingo intent on raiding your camp while your guide is away? Are you right to be worried? Find out in the next chapter.

ANSWERS from page 60

1. True.

2. False. A wallaroo is another type of kangaroo.

3. True. Their teeth wear out.

4. True. The saliva evaporates and cools blood just under the skin.

5. True.

6. False. Totally. They eat grass.

Chapter 7
BUSH TUCKER
AND
BOOMERANGS

Dark.

   Alone.

      Night-time Sound FX:

         Dog barking (?) behind camp.

           (Could it be a dingo?)

Are there large dangerous animals around here? How would they react to you?

Some Australians react rather strangely when confronted with a big dangerous animal like you. Turn the page and match the animal to its reaction when it gets stressed out.

Animal	How it reacts
1. Goanna	a. Attempts to scare you away by umbrellaing out the skin around its neck.
2. Frilled lizard	b. Charges and savages you with its vicious tusks.
3. Red kangaroo	c. Rakes you with its hind feet.
4. Wild pig	d. Thinks you are a tree and climbs up.

Answers on page 70

Wild Pigs! They aren't Australian. What are they doing here? They are farm pigs that have escaped and bred – gone **feral!** They have adapted well to life out in the bush and over the years have become lean and mean, rather like the wild boars they are descended from . . . and they are a pest. Wild pigs eat just about anything – nesting birds, young animals like kangaroos, even farmers' lambs. They trample and ruin delicate vegetation around billabongs and pollute them with their poo. And, because they are cunning and breed so fast, attempts to wipe them out by hunting them have been unsuccessful.

Pigs aren't the only problem. Here are some other feral animals that you could find in the Australian bush.

- **Mice and rabbits** that have multiplied to plague proportions, destroying crops and bush land.
- **Cats.** Moggies gone wild are driving small native possums and bandicoots to the brink of extinction. So are the descendants of foxes that English people released because they thought it would be good to have something familiar to hunt.
- **Water buffalo**
- **Camels**
- **Horses** (called brumbies)

And . . . er . . . dingoes. Yes. These are not native marsupials. They are most likely the descendents of the hunting dogs that were first brought to Australia when the original aboriginal people arrived.

DINGO

That barking. You could swear it's nearer now. There's some rustling in the bushes.

69

ANSWERS from page 68

1. d. Goannas will often try and keep themselves between the source of danger and a tree that they can run up if necessary. If one thinks you are a tree, the best thing you can do is to lie down. If you get too close to a goanna, most likely the first thing it will do is to stand high on its legs and give out a low-pitched hiss – it's trying to make itself look bigger to scare you away.

2. a. If one's resting on a tree trunk, it just keeps moving around so you're on the opposite side of the tree. It might instead avoid the confrontation by running away on its hind feet, dinosaur-style. Note: You won't see any frilled lizards in the dry season as they usually find hollow logs to hibernate in.

3. c. Though far more likely to bound away from you, male kangaroos and wallaroos have been known to lean back on their tails and rake forward with their feet. The long central toenails have been known to inflict serious injuries, particularly to farmers' dogs that have harassed them. Note: kangaroos hurt far more people indirectly when people accidentally crash into them (usually at night) in their cars.

4. b. Wild pigs can inflict nasty injuries, though, as with most animals, are more likely to flee the scene rather than tangle with a big, nasty human being.

How would you like your ants? Lemon-flavoured?

Cameron's greeting out of the stillness of the night makes you jump nearly out of your skin.

Woof! Woof!

"Just a barking owl," Cameron gestures over his shoulders. "Dingoes don't bark, they just yip and yelp. And they'd only go for you if you were really helpless."

"Or they were really hungry," he adds with a chuckle. "So, these ants . . ."

Green tree-ants. Available all over the northern bush country. Bite into their bums for an acid lemon tang. (It helps to have a bit of saliva in your mouth first as you can burn your tongue. And be careful how you pick up your ants. They bite.)

Actually, green tree-ants are not so much a food but a flavouring. Traditionally, aborigines in the Northern Territory would add them to meals of edible roots, which tasted rather bitter at the start of the wet season. Also, their nests, which are made of clusters of leaves glued together with spider-like silk exuded from the ant grubs, can be boiled up to make medicinal tea . . . a sort of ants' nest tea bag.

Here are some other bush tucker foods. Match them up to where you would find them and how you would eat them.

What?	Where?	How?
1. Witchetty grubs	A. Surface of eucalyptus leaves.	W. Pop straight into your mouth – a buttery-tasting ball of protein (also said to be good lightly fried).
2. Honey ant	B. Fairly common in open and wooded country.	X. Scrape it off with your fingernails and eat raw.
3. Goanna	C. In the roots of witchetty bushes and blood oaks (you can tell these by their blood red sap).	Y. Suck their big bums.
4. Lerp scale	D. Under tree roots (limited availability – selected desert areas only).	Z. Cook whole in its skin.

Answers on page 74

So which edible delights has Cameron brought for you? Just some hairy wizened roots, a type of bush potato which he can roast in the embers of the fire. He's also found some *witchetty grubs*. Pop them in your mouth and enjoy their creaminess.

Bush tucker. All this knowledge of what's edible in the Outback has been built up over thousands of years by aboriginal people. They also developed some ruthlessly efficient ways of hunting.

Look at the pictures of these traditional aboriginal weapons and see if you can match them to their use.

Hunting Weapon	Used to hunt	Range	What it does to your prey
1. Throwing stick (sticks just gathered, crudely cut and used for hunting)	A. Larger birds like ducks and geese	D. Short	G. Kills outright; (The prey could hurt you if it were just wounded.)
2. Boomerang	B. Kangaroo	E. Medium	H. Swoops low and knocks away the legs of your prey from under it.
3. Spear and Woomera	C. Small birds	F. Long	I. Flies on a straight path and stuns or kills.

Answers on page 75

ANSWERS from page 72

1. C, W.

2. D,Y.   These are actually specially adapted females
         that store food (energy) as sugar for the rest
         of the colony.

3. B, Z Note: Aborigines traditionally never used
         cooking pots, though some coastal groups
         sometimes made use of large seashells.

4. A, X.   These white blotches on leaves are the nests
         for tiny pinkish grubs. They have a vaguely
         sugary, eucalyptus taste.

Throwing Sticks come in a variety of shapes and sizes but the
basic idea is that they fly straight and stun the prey.

Boomerangs are flat on one (the lower) side and curved on the
other so that they generate a lift force as they spin - much like
helicopter rotorblades do. Throw them low to the ground and
they swerve up into the animal or bird being hunted. Some
hooked types are meant to bounce off the ground and then
swoop up into their target. Hunting

boomerangs do not come back. That sort had more of a ritual use. To get your boomerang to return, throw it at roughly 45 degrees against the wind direction with the flat side of the boomerang against your hand. You might need to give it some spin when you let go. Getting your boomerang to come back takes practice. If you try to catch it, use both hands to clap it to a halt (catching a boomerang with one hand can hurt or even break your fingers). Note: not all tribes of aborigines used boomerangs.

Spears have always been used throughout Australia for hunting larger animals like kangaroos. Traditionally these often had hard wooden tips but in the early twentieth century, as telegraph lines were being put up through the bush country, many aborigines found that the glazed ceramic insulators that the wires were hung from could be chipped into much sharper points. (People travelling overland were asked to look for breaks in the wires and repair any that they found!) These days, many spears have metal points.

To make your spear fly faster and farther, use a woomera spear thrower. This stick, hooked at both ends, has the

ANSWERS from page 73

1. C, D, I.   2. A, E, H.   3. B, F, G.

effect of lengthening your throwing arm and giving extra leverage. Using a woomera an experienced hunter can throw a spear 180 metres or more.

It's not quite light when Cameron nudges you from your slumber. He is pointing towards the ridge with the slanted, painted rock. With stiff limbs from sleeping on the hard ground, you crawl out of your swag, grab your camera and stumble after your friend as he scurries up the slope, bent low to the ground, sticking to every available patch of cover. His movement is almost silent. Yours is not and you can see Cameron grimace each time you dislodge a rock or snap some twig underfoot. Finally you pant up to where Cameron has squatted behind some low bushes overlooking a shallow stony valley beyond the rocks. You see what your guide's stealth was all about. There, below you in the dawn half-light are three rabbit-sized animals. They are sitting upright like wallabies and are looking towards you. Scarcely daring to breathe for fear of spooking the animals, you raise your camera and press the shutter release, snapping off four shots in quick succession before - oh, no - the film's out! And the auto rewind sets in. If they hadn't heard you before, they certainly have now. The wallabies set off, speeding forwards in small bounds with long tails that bob up and down in time with their hopping. The strange thing is, they don't hop like any wallabies you have seen before. These ones always land right foot first!

Chapter 8
FINLAYSON'S RAT-KANGAROO

1931: The Stony Deserts of South West Queensland.

Hedley Herbert Finlayson was astonished. Even galloping at full pelt on horseback, he and his men could not catch up with the little critters that they had come to study. With relays of fresh horses, they chased one poor animal for 20 kilometres across sand ridges and stony plains, exhausting it nearly to death before they could catch it. Luckily for the group, they had Butcher, an aboriginal guide. When he said he could catch an oolacunta with his bare hands the others jeered at him. But Butcher carried on with his plan, reckoning that the place where the explorers had first spotted the marsupials was most likely to be their home. So, when Finlayson and his cronies set off after yet another one, he did the logical thing – he doubled back and searched around for burrows. When the horsemen came back empty-handed again, Butcher held out a bag, tied at the top. Inside there was a fully grown adult and a young joey. As he had already done with the other exhausted ones he had run down and caught, Finlayson measured this oolacunta and noted down its colour and weight. Pretty soon he realised that the animal he was dealing with had to be the desert rat-kangaroo, a small wallaby that been discovered in another patch of dry country by another explorer nearly ninety years before and then never seen since (by scientists and explorers, that is, not the local aborigines, for whom seeing one was no special event). Finlayson went back to Adelaide with news of his 'discovery', returning over the next two years to study the animals. But when he went back in 1935, the oolacuntas had gone.

Years went by with no sightings. Desert rat-kangaroos were presumed extinct, possibly wiped out by cats or foxes or forced into the least hospitable areas of the deserts, as all the good land was used for cattle or sheep farming.

But now there is a doubt. It looks like you've proved everyone wrong. Those photos in your camera show that the *oolacunta* does indeed live. More than that, you can show that there are lots left; isn't that a whole mob of them that you can see on the brow of that hill over there? You twist your camera's zoom lens to maximum magnification and snap off some more shots with a new film you've just put in. You know there's no point chasing the animals for a better view. They could easily outrun (outhop) you. Even chasing them in Ulysses would probably be pointless; even if you could keep up with them over the rough ground, you're trying to study them, not exhaust them to an early grave.

Lucky for you then that you've got Cameron. And look what he's hit upon! Wrapped in an old blanket, is an *oolacunta* that he's caught unharmed with his

bare hands. How did he do it? Just like the man in the story, he beams. He just reached down some holes.

Quickly, so the animal doesn't get distressed, you take some measurements and a few close-up photos, which will be all you need to prove the desert rat-kangaroo still exists. Then you release it to hop off in its lopsided right-foot-forward way back to its mates on the hilltop.
You and Cameron have done it. You've rediscovered a species long thought extinct and you have photos and data to prove it! The *oolacunta* is clearly going to need further

study. You'd hate to think of it going missing for another ninety years before someone rediscovers it. The Morangie Rocks area will need looking after and who could be better than Cameron and others from his tribe who've already been doing that for centuries? But to get all of this done you will need publicity. You'll have to get your story in the papers. You'll have to get yourself on TV. Who knows? There may even be a bit-part in the world-famous Aussie soap opera *next-doorers* . . .

When you get back . . .

You're still out in the bush, remember. There's an awful lot of ground to cover before you get anywhere near a tarmac road, let alone *home*. You had better figure out how you are going to do it. Look at this map of your route and work out the way you got here.

- Your adventure started with you nearly being mown down by a road train.
- You passed magnetic termite mounds and avoided a bush fire on your way to . . .
- The Burrumbarroo wetlands where you . . .
- Crossed Nellie's Creek and . . .
- Traversed the plains towards Morangie Rocks . . .
- Finally, in a valley beyond, you discovered the rat-kangaroo.

Answer on page 84

83

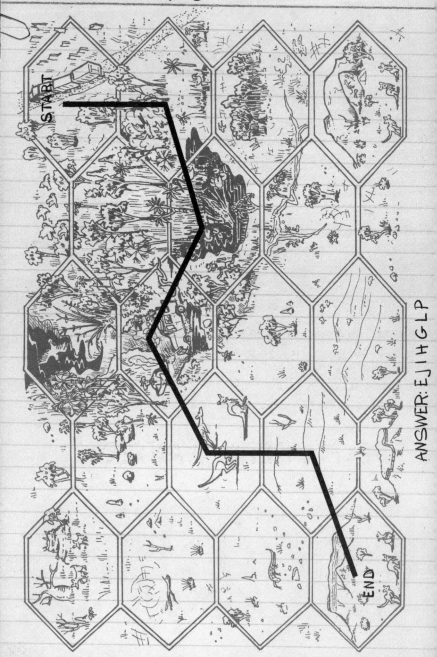

ANSWER: EJIHGLP

You've survived the harsh Australian Outback and proved yourself as an expert explorer. What challenge will you take up next? Have you thought of exploring **Under the Sea** or climbing the high **Himalayas**? How about travelling into **Deepest Borneo**? Whichever you choose...

EXPLORERS WANTED!

About the author

Writer and broadcaster, Simon Chapman, is a self-confessed jungle addict, making expeditions whenever he can. His travels have taken him to tropical forests all over the world, from Borneo and Irian Jaya to the Amazon.

The story of his search for a mythical Giant Ape in the Bolivian rainforest, *The Monster of the Madidi*, was published in 2001. He has also had numerous articles and illustrations published in magazines in Britain and the US, including *Wanderlust*, *BBC Wildlife* and *South American Explorer*, and has written and recorded for BBC Radio 4, and lectured on the organisation of jungle expeditions at the Royal Geographical Society, of which he is a fellow.

When not exploring, Simon lives with his wife and his two young children in Lancaster, where he teaches physics in a high school.

EXPLORERS WANTED!

CALLING ALL
EXPLORERS!

We hope that you've enjoyed this **EXPLORERS WANTED!** adventure.

To help us make our next books even more exciting, we'd love to hear from you. We want you to tell us what you liked best about this book, and which places you think **EXPLORERS WANTED!** should go in the future.

In return, you'll receive a limited-edition **EXPLORERS WANTED!** badge to show off to your friends and news about the series, author events that Simon Chapman is involved in and fantastic competitions and give-aways.

Send your ideas and comments to:
Simon Chapman
c/o Publicity Department
Egmont Books Limited
239 Kensington High Street
London W8 6SA

www.explorerswanted.co.uk

More **EXPLORERS WANTED!**
titles for you to collect!